Gratitude at Home

How to practise gratitude with your child

© 2016 RICHARD DANIEL CURTIS

Copyright © 2016 Richard Daniel Curtis (founder of The Kid Calmer Ltd)

Cover Design, Interior Formatting and Book Publishing by:
Chrystel Melhuish from Plum Design & Publishing Ltd
www.plumdesignpublishing.com

All Rights Reserved. No part of this publication may be reproduced, stored in or introduced into a retrieval system, or transmitted, in any form, or by any means without the prior written permission of the publisher.

The right of Richard Daniel Curtis to be identified as author of this work has been asserted in accordance with sections 77 and 78 of the Copyright Designs and Patents Act 1988.

This book is sold subject to the condition that it shall not, by way of trade or otherwise, be lent, re-sold, hired out or otherwise circulated in any form, binding or cover other than that in which it is published and without a similar condition including this condition being imposed on the subsequent purchaser.

ISBN-13: 978-1-912010-07-3

Published in December 2016 by: The Kid Calmer Ltd
www.thekidcalmer.com

....

This book and the series of accompanying Gratitude Journals for children and young people came to life through the joint efforts of Richard Daniel Curtis, leading behaviour expert and Chrystel Melhuish's existing journals on Gratitude. Their work was the perfect synergy to bring Gratitude into schools and homes with the vision of helping millions of children around the world feeling happier and more fulfilled in life.

For the accompanying Gratitude Journal at Home Books, check out:
www.inspiringjournals.com

For complimentary extra hints, tips and resources, then please sign up at www.gratitudeforchildren.com

If your child's school would be a great place to practise Gratitude, then check out our Gratitude in Schools Series at www.inspiringjournals.com

WHAT OTHER PARENTS SAY ABOUT THIS BOOK

"I really loved this book. It has certainly made me want to get started on the practice of Gratitude with my daughters, who are 9 and 14. It provides a great base from which to build on, a reason for quality time with your children and provides them with a fantastic life skill!"

Amanda Rees

....

"As a mother who's recently started to practise Gratitude myself, reading this book has not only allowed me to share my practice with my two children, but to develop a routine with them that is perfect for their age.

When I read this book, I knew from the benefits, the explanations, the ideas, the questions answered that Gratitude was perfect for my family and I knew just how to start."

Adele Bryant

....

"I am a big advocate of practising Gratitude however this is the first guide I have read written specifically to help parents teach their children the practice. What a fabulous idea. I do encourage my children to practise Gratitude however if I'm absolutely honest we've not being doing it consistently and with a 3 year age gap between my girls, what works for one daughter hasn't worked for the other.

I love that Richard has shared different approaches to use depending on the age of your child. I also found it very useful to show my children the Gratitude journal examples – sometimes when you first start practising Gratitude, it's difficult to know what to say. This gives you a fabulous foundation to start and continue the practice of Gratitude."

Sherry Bevan, Author of The Confident Mother

"I love your book! I wish my parents would have read this book when I was a child. Gratitude is a true gift and your book is a practical guide in the 'how' for parents. I love how you have addressed different ages and stages in a child's development. As a parent and a child psychologist, I must say this is a valuable addition to my library."

Dr Karen Monster-Peters

....

"I am so pleased to find a book on this topic as I truly believe that Gratitude is an essential skill all kids should develop. The age related content helped me to understand the developmental stage they go through and how that affects their positivity and attitude. The step-by-step guide made it easy to implement and put in place.

I cannot wait to use the techniques with my boys (age 6 and 12) and I am looking forward to seeing the benefits it brings them. I hope they make it a habit for life!"

Lucinda Dawes

....

"As a single mother of two kids (a daughter aged 3 and son aged 6) going through divorce I have found great insight on how to guide these two precious souls towards learning and applying some Gratitude techniques. The last year has been a roller coaster ride for all of us and throughout all the pain being grateful for them has kept me literally alive.

I love these beautiful, age appropriate and practical examples and tools on how to teach and practise Gratitude with our children. Helping our children learn Gratitude will make them realise that they are not the victims of this situation, but that we have so much to be grateful for and that our past is just a story. Thank you for reminding us that focusing on the good ... now... is all that matters.

Gratitude is an instant feel good for all - as you explain so nicely in your latest book."

Rolandi Bouwer

"Thank you so much for introducing this topic with children and focusing on helping us parents teach our children the wonderful world of Gratitude! I love how you've laid out step by step instructions on how to integrate this practice into our everyday lives!

It was so easy to read and flowed well. I'm so excited to start this practice with my 2 daughters! I have a toddler and when I put her to bed at night, I whisper in her ear all the wonderful things she loves in this world or tell her to think about all the fun we had earlier that day so I see I've been practising this with her all along! I also have an 11 year old daughter who is in puberty now and seems down and doesn't share much so this will hopefully be a special thing we can do together that will hopefully bring us closer and help her look at the bright side of life."

Cummins Mabry

....

"We have been really enjoying putting into practice the techniques mentioned. The book is really clear, easy to find the appropriate age section and enjoyable to follow. I know it will have a positive effect on the rest of their lives if they truly embed the practice of Gratitude."

Becky Cook

....

"Wow, I'm so grateful for this book. Believe you I needed to be reminded about the importance of Gratitude myself. I'm glad to have landed this in my hands. My life will never be the same again.

We are starting our 1st daily Gratitude with my kids today. Just when I was asking assistance on how to get my kids to start appreciate everything that happens in life, this book dropped into my life - wow! Thank you so much for living your purpose because more and more families will be revived because of you. Thank you!"

Portia Zwane

CONTENTS

WHAT OTHER PARENTS SAY ABOUT THIS BOOK 3

INTRODUCTION 9

ABOUT THIS BOOK 11

WHAT IS GRATITUDE? 12

FAMOUS PEOPLE WHO HAVE SPOKEN ABOUT GRATITUDE 13

THE IMPACT OF GRATITUDE 14

WHAT IS A GRATITUDE JOURNAL? 15

THE ATMOSPHERE FOR GRATITUDE 16

THE TRICKS THE BRAIN WILL PLAY ON YOU 18

HELPING SOMEONE LET GO OF THEIR THOUGHTS 19

THE DEVELOPMENT OF A CHILD'S REFLECTIVE CAPACITY 20

EXAMPLES OF GRATITUDE JOURNAL ENTRIES 22

INTRODUCING GRATITUDE TO CHILDREN UNDER 2 28

INTRODUCING GRATITUDE TO CHILDREN AGED 2-5 32

INTRODUCING GRATITUDE TO CHILDREN AGED 5-7 38

INTRODUCING GRATITUDE TO CHILDREN AGED 8-12 44

INTRODUCING GRATITUDE TO YOUNG TEENAGERS (13-15 YEARS OLD) 50

INTRODUCING GRATITUDE TO TEENAGERS 15 AND OLDER 56

THANK YOU 62

ABOUT THE AUTHOR 63

INTRODUCTION

Thank you for introducing Gratitude to your child, I know they will be grateful too. I hope that you find many helpful ideas and information in this book to help inspire, motivate and celebrate the many things in the life of your child.

I wish that I had discovered the practice of Gratitude when I was still teaching in the classroom, I know it would have changed my practice massively and had a huge impact for the children I taught. I would have loved to have discovered Gratitude when I was working with children with extreme behaviour problems, I know they would have benefited from the daily routine.

I actually didn't discover Gratitude until I was struggling with the daily habit of finishing my fourth book. I had been ill with tonsillitis, which had made me incredibly tired and I was also heavily consumed by the development of several qualifications for working with young people. Someone suggested to me that I try a new morning routine, try 20 minutes of physical exercise, 20 minutes of Gratitude and 20 minutes of learning something new.

This new habit has led to me getting up very early in order to make sure that I do it every day and I am thankful for the impact it has had in my life. When I was asked to think about how you could teach this habit to children I was delighted and set to work straight away. Imagine the impact of being able to practise Gratitude with them, how it would teach healthy habits that would help their emotional wellbeing.

So here it is, your guide to teaching your child about Gratitude. This book contains an introduction to Gratitude, a brief summary of the impact of practising Gratitude and some ideas about how to introduce the habit to the different ages. Please remember, as with any behavioural change, that to make it a true daily habit, it will take on average 66 days for it to become embedded into a daily routine.

Thank you on behalf of your child. I know that they will benefit from your actions.

With Gratitude,
Richard Daniel Curtis

P.S. For the accompanying Gratitude Journal at Home Books, check out:
www.inspiringjournals.com

P.P.S. If you'd like complimentary extra hints, tips and resources, then please sign up at **www.gratitudeforchildren.com**

P.P.P.S: If your child's school would be a great place to practise Gratitude, then check out my Gratitude in Schools books at **www.inspiringjournals.com**

ABOUT THIS BOOK

In this book you will find ideas to help introduce your child to the concept of Gratitude and how to take their first steps. Whilst the habit itself should continue on as a part of daily life (or at least three times a week), the initial teaching of the habit can be a barrier for some. Included are a series of small introductory steps to help introduce how to recognise what Gratitude is and how to take these first few steps.

It contains an explanation of how Gratitude fits in with their development at that stage, how to explain Gratitude to your child, some activities to introduce it and some ideas to help you continue to form the habit.

If you have more than one child, then Gratitude can be practised together or separately. This will depend on your children; however, it will be important for them that they perceive they receive fair treatment. Fair is obviously not always equal; you may need to spend longer time wise with a young child than with an older child for example. However, explain the need to the older child or get them involved in supporting the younger one and you will quickly overcome their protestations of "it's not fair." The important thing is that the practice of Gratitude is a positive special time, whether just with you or as a family – I promise you will learn lots about your child!

For complimentary ideas, resources and to share with other parents and carers using Gratitude, please visit **www.gratitudeforchildren.com**.

WHAT IS GRATITUDE?

Gratitude is the practice of expressing thanks for the things in a person's life that they are appreciative for. This act of showing appreciation for the many wonderful things in a person's life help them to feel more positive and help counteract the negativity in the world around us.

Gratitude can take different forms, some like to write a letter, some keep a diary, others a journal, some write them on paper and put them in a jar and others say them out loud. Most people who show appreciation do so regularly, often daily. They set aside small amounts of time to express thanks for the positives in their lives, the little things that they appreciate, the small rays of light in a sometimes very negative world. Some do this in the evening, others first thing in the morning.

Gratitude is particularly helpful at times when someone is experiencing difficulties or feeling low. At these times it helps to remind the person of the positives in their lives and to focus on them. It helps to ensure our mood remains positive even in the face of adversity.

The practice of Gratitude dates back thousands of years and has been linked to the ancient Greeks and early Christianity. In recent years there have been a number of clinical studies researching the impact of Gratitude and appreciative acts. Some very successful people use Gratitude as a habit, more than may be realised. They may or may not talk about it, but they will be the people who you see appreciate the acts of other people. Gratitude really does change lives.

FAMOUS PEOPLE WHO HAVE SPOKEN ABOUT GRATITUDE

Many successful people acknowledge the importance of Gratitude in their lives, they see it as important to reflect on the positives in their lives or write thank you notes. For example, Douglas Conant of Campbell Soup estimates he wrote 30,000 thank you notes whilst there.

Others who have spoken about practising Gratitude include:
- Dr Wayne Dyer
- Dr Joe Vitale
- Dr Deepak Chopra
- Louise Hay
- Chris Pratt
- Will Arnett
- Kelsey Grammar
- Matt Damon
- Jerry Seinfeld
- Clint Eastwood
- Oprah Winfrey
- Dalai Lama
- JFK
- Willie Nelson
- Robin Sharma
- Roger Hamilton
- Mark Zuckerberg
- Jimmy Fallon
- Jack Welch.

THE IMPACT OF GRATITUDE

There are a number of benefits of practising Gratitude on a regular basis, these include:
- Less stress
- More accepting of social difficulties
- More forgiving
- More generous
- Greater joy and pleasure in activities
- Closer to friends and family
- Improved ability to cope with life challenges.

In addition to the above, the University of California, in their study of more than 1,000 people (aged 8-80) who practise regular Gratitude, report health benefits too:
- Longer sleep
- More regular exercise
- Lower blood pressure
- Reduced impact of aches and pains
- Stronger immune systems.

A 1998 study by McCraty et al showed a reduction in the cortisol (stress) level in the body after cultivating appreciative thoughts. Seligman, Steen, and Peterson in 2005 reported a month's worth of elevated happiness after writing one thank you letter.

WHAT IS A GRATITUDE JOURNAL?

A Gratitude Journal is a special book to keep a record of Gratitude in. It is a book to be treated with respect as it reminds the owner of all of the positive things in their lives.

If used as part of a morning routine, it helps the owner to set their emotional level for the day. People's minds wake up in different moods and just the way they are woken can have an impact on their approach to the day. Focusing on the positives in their lives helps them to ensure that they are in charge of their emotions throughout the day.

When used as part of the evening routine, it can help to reflect on the day and settle the mind in a positive state prior to sleep.

When times are hard, it can help to revisit previous pages of the Gratitude Journal to remind the brain of the wonderful things in their lives. The number of things entered into a Gratitude Journal can range from just one a day to several hundred, just as long as they are truly thankful for them.

THE ATMOSPHERE FOR GRATITUDE

Gratitude is best practised daily in a dedicated time. It should be viewed as part of the daily routine, whether that is in the morning or later in the day. This helps the brain to subconsciously register the importance and helps to make it more likely to be transferred into daily life.

Beginning a Gratitude session should be calming, to allow the body and mind to settle and be in the moment. This momentary state of contentment helps the brain to release all of its regular thoughts and focus on the positive aspects it is expressing.

Closing the eyes and taking a few slow deep breaths prior to commencing Gratitude, it is common to feel a physical shift in the body. This feeling can be strange at first and it is important to warn young people to expect it. With more practice in Gratitude, these are experienced more regularly, a subconscious sign of positivity.

It is common, even for expert practitioners, to find the brain wandering onto trains of thoughts brought on by the Gratitude process. As the mind is conscious that this is happening, it is important to let that thought train be stored for later and the brain refocused on the Gratitude. Children (or even adults) may find themselves distracted by these thoughts. They originate as a result of the clearing of the mind and the clarity it is experiencing. It may help to jot these thoughts on a list as Gratitude is going on, so that they are out of the mind and it is free to continue to pursue appreciative thoughts.

The time itself should be relaxed, unhurried and relatively peaceful. Conversation is allowed between you and your child, but needs to be focussed on the Gratitude.

Ending a Gratitude session should not be a hurried affair to get everything down before the time is up. Instead, with practice it becomes a time to be grateful for the amount of Gratitude that the individual has achieved. As they approach the end of the time they have set aside, encourage them to take a step back in their minds and see what they have accomplished in that session.

For someone who struggles with identifying their Special Moment of the Day, it may help them to think about a time in the day that they felt strong emotions or that they wish to remember.

Initially, allow at least 20 minutes whilst the concept and the habit are introduced. As time passes this time will begin to reduce to being a regular 10 minutes. However, many people choose to keep the longer period of time and set themselves harder Gratitude targets, such as starting with a minimum of 25 Gratitudes.

Expect to feel a sense of enjoyment and satisfaction as you and your child become more used to the practice of Gratitude. It can be quite fun and as time goes on you look forward to it, especially on those days when we are feeling down, stressed or blue. The practice of Gratitude really does pick you up!

THE TRICKS THE BRAIN WILL PLAY ON YOU

One of the big reasons that people don't continue on with Gratitude long term is their brain. The brain is a curious thing and will often try to sabotage the things we are trying to achieve.

For example, whenever it can be negative or pessimistic about something it will be. In fact, babies are born with the ability to cry, be frustrated, be angry, but they have to learn to smile. Humans actually have to learn not just how to smile, they have to learn to be happy, to be content and to occupy themselves.

So given the opportunity the brain will try to revert to a negative state and it takes the conscience to positively overcome that.

As people try to build in new habits, the brain initially opposes this change and will do anything it can to sabotage the plan. Resistance increases over the first few weeks and the brain tries to divert the mind onto other things, or even tells the mind how much it must hate doing this new thing, that it's hard and why doesn't the mind just give up.

Only after the mind has won this battle will the brain start to accept that this is the new habit and begin wiring it in as a long term habit. This process can take some time!

HELPING SOMEONE LET GO OF THEIR THOUGHTS

An important part of the practice of Gratitude is emptying the mind and letting the stresses of life go during those few minutes. This can very hard for even experienced practitioners, let alone the young.

There are a number of different methods that people may use to achieve this. Many of these techniques rely on picturing or imagining the thoughts and all of them depend on the ability to reflect on our thoughts:
- Some spend 30 seconds writing down the things they are currently thinking about prior to starting Gratitude, so that they can come back to them when they finish.
- Others visualise their thoughts as a number of balloons and imagine themselves cutting each one free or releasing them; watching them fly off into the distance.
- Imagining their thoughts on a cloud and slowly blowing it away.
- Focusing on an object in detail, so much so that other thoughts cannot intrude.
- Some have an imaginary box in their minds where they pack their thoughts away whilst they do their Gratitude.

Throughout this book a balloon visualisation exercise has been used, but it is recommended to share the other methods as time goes on, so that your child can find their preferred method.

THE DEVELOPMENT OF A CHILD'S REFLECTIVE CAPACITY

The way the mind develops from birth until after adolescence affects the way that Gratitude is used.

During the early years of a child's life, until the age of 3 or 4, a child's life is centred about meeting their own needs. Apart from food and drink, this also affects our early social interactions with adults and other children, where primarily the focus is on the child being entertained or controlling others. Behaviour during this stage of a child's life is very much a bid to achieve a result and tantrums are a frequent result of being thwarted.

As a child grows socially, they learn to cooperate with others to achieve a goal. Play extends from being self-focussed to seeking a common goal and will often be focussed around games with shared rules (for example homes, doctors, school, vets, a particular TV programme the friends are all familiar with) so that the group can focus on the game rather than needing to learn the rules. Children will be heard to be talking about their play or the game as it happens, almost like a running commentary. From the age of 4 years old until about 7, a child is learning the importance of getting on with others and overcoming the complexities of maintaining friendships with other children. Motivation for behaviour during this stage remains a bid to achieve something, however children can struggle to verbalise their original intention or reason for an action when asked to do so by an adult.

At around the age of 7 or 8 years old, a child's external commentary disappears. At this stage it has begun to be internalised and so continues inside their heads – it is not unheard of for a child at this age to complain about the voice in their head. Play becomes more complex as the friendship group learns to adapt the nature of their play so that it no longer focuses on play with shared rules. As the friendship group are able to understand each other's viewpoints, they can adapt the play in their heads to embed new rules (for example playing their friend's family's rules for Monopoly rather than their own). This is the developmental stage where children have the cognitive skills to reflect on their own actions and be able to think through the different choices they have. The monologue that accompanied their play begins to become a dialogue in their heads, adding in different voices as they become more aware of difference. Over time these voices develop into what is known as our conscience.

From around the age of 10 years old, the brain is preparing for puberty and so is growing millions of new neurons. This is a time of growth for the child's emerging personality as their brain enjoys experiencing as many new activities as possible.

The reflective mind enters reverse gear with the onset of puberty. As the brain closes down many functions of the frontal lobe in preparation for the rewiring process it is undertaking, one of the skills commonly lost is that of reflective capacity. The primate areas of the brain are responsible for the brain during this period of a teenager's life and so it is common to see more emotional responses, riskier behaviour and less capacity in dealing with life's challenges. For many teenagers this internal struggle with their emotions can cause an overload and may possibly lead to depression. Reflection may be difficult at this time, so habits, like Gratitude, help the teenage brain cope with this difficult time.

As the teenager emerges from the end of puberty, the frontal lobes begin to be used again and reflective capacity returns. At this point the teenager develops their own belief systems, independent of any views of their parents for the first time in their lives. As they go about their first few steps into adulthood, they gain new insights into previous actions and learning, often expressing Gratitude for things that happened in their lives many years previously.

Examples of Gratitude Journal Entries

EXAMPLE 1

Date: Monday 5th September

Today I am grateful for...

1. My mum

2. My cat, Smudge, who always strokes herself against me when I'm in my room

3. My phone

4. My favourite Artemis Fowl books

5. My bike

Special moment of the day...
How did I feel? ♥

When I woke up in the morning with Smudge curled up under my arm. It made me feel so warm and content, I didn't want to get up. I wanted that happy feeling to last forever.

Download this example from www.gratitudeforchildren.com

EXAMPLE 2

Date: Tuesday 6th September

Today I am grateful for...

1. Going out at the weekend and getting a milkshake

2. A hot bath

3. Playing with my cat

4. When I put on loud music and dance around my bedroom – I love this!

5. When I am with my friends and we just can't stop laughing, George always starts by making me laugh

Special moment of the day...
How did I feel? ♥

Today I completed the last level of World of Warcraft, it's taken me three weeks and to finally finish it was amazing. I felt like I had mastered the game and was so proud of myself, I felt on top of the world!

Download this example from www.gratitudeforchildren.com

EXAMPLE 3

Date: Wednesday 7th September

Today I am grateful for...

1. Things that make me laugh

2. Taking a shower after a long day

3. Eating my favourite meal

4. That feeling you get when you are with your best friends and you are doing something together

5. My thick duvet when it's cold

Special moment of the day...
How did I feel? ♥

After we'd finished for the day, me and my friends went down to the café for hot chocolate and cheesy chips. We bought the cheesy chips together and shared them. Later Zdenka came and joined us and we had to catch her up with all of the gossip. I felt like we were a group who really liked each other and I didn't want that feeling to end.

Download this example from www.gratitudeforchildren.com

EXAMPLE 4

Date: Thursday 8th September

Today I am grateful for...

1. Hobbies

2. Looking forward to the future

3. Possibilities

4. Companionship

5. Contentment

Special moment of the day...
How did I feel? ♥

When I was with my mates and my girlfriend was there. She was joining in with us and had her arm around me. She was laughing as much as I was at the things that Andy has been doing. I felt like I was loved and happy surrounded by my friends.

Download this example from www.gratitudeforchildren.com

EXAMPLE 5

Date: Friday 9th September

Today I am grateful for...

1. Love

2. Inspiration

3. Joy

4. Failure

5. Satisfaction

Special moment of the day...
How did I feel? ♥

Spending time listening to my mum as she needed someone to talk to. I enjoyed being there for her and could understand her feelings and frustration. It reminded me of some of my friends and the problems they have. I enjoyed being able to help her out, it's not something I've done before, it made me feel proud.

Download this example from www.gratitudeforchildren.com

INTRODUCING GRATITUDE TO CHILDREN UNDER 2

INTRODUCTION

Gratitude at this young age is not necessarily about saying thank you, it relates more to understanding what activities they enjoy. From infant upwards children learn to connect positive experiences to a release of endorphins in their brains. In fact, this is actually how we learn to smile: the reaction of parents to a baby pulling a smile gives the baby's brain a huge rush of the feel-good hormone. As this happens more and more regularly, they learn that when they feel good they smile and when they smile it helps them to feel good.

By helping your child to recognise the things they enjoy and like, you are teaching them the underlying skills needed for later Gratitude. A huge part of Gratitude is the ability to recognise things you are thankful for and that begins with recognising they are enjoying an activity.

EXPLAINING GRATITUDE TO YOUR CHILD

As we have discussed, at this age you are unlikely to explain Gratitude, instead the important skill you will need to teach your child is to recognise the activities they like doing.

This begins whilst they are infants and is learnt from the reactions of those around us. These reactions trigger an endorphin rush that the infant brain relates to the activity being done at the time. These connections are formed and the baby starts to relate different activities to particular adults. Some of these games are then transferred to other adults and the infant recognises that these are games that can be played with anyone.

As they become mobile then they start to choose to play these games on their own or take them to the adults to play. It is important for play development and later Gratitude that these are met with an endorphin releasing reaction by the adults to teach their growing brain a sense of satisfaction with doing the activities.

This begins to become an internal process as the portable baby begins to select toys to play with themselves. The initial satisfaction is short lived and so parental focus should shift onto teaching the child to extend that play beyond a few fleeting seconds.

A part of this life skill is learning how to deal with extending play independently and avoiding boredom. Rather than let technology, such as TV or tablets, entertain a child whilst the adult is busy, it can be more effective to let them practise the skills you were teaching them in the previous stage. Congratulate and reward your child with praise as you see them extend their play on their own. This again helps them to feel the satisfaction of avoiding the boredom and entertaining themselves.

ACTIVITIES TO INTRODUCE GRATITUDE

For a young infant face to face games are ideal for teaching enjoyment of activities. Simple peek-a-boo games allow the parent to express facial expressions that the infant will begin to copy.

Saying 'thank you' as you play these games helps to teach it as a language pattern associated with enjoying activities. As your child begins to talk or communicate using baby sign language, then teach them to say 'thank you' after playing a game.

Once a child becomes mobile, help them to choose between toys to play with you. As they choose a toy, say thank you and ensure they experience that endorphin rush whilst they're playing that game.

Over time, adapt this to asking your child to get a toy they like playing with. Repeat the expression of Gratitude, encouraging your child to say or sign 'thank you' when you finish playing.

As they approach 18 months to 2 years, children should be able to recognise the games they like playing with and show other people. This expression of self-awareness should again be met with positivity from the adults so that they learn that expression of things they enjoy is okay.

MOVING FORWARD

At this early stage in a child's life the steps you are taking are laying the foundations for a future where they will be able to recognise things they enjoy, express Gratitude for them and also see the positive things in life.

Keep the daily habits going and keep expressing Gratitude in front of them, so they become a part of your child's life that they don't even think they do. This habit helps them to learn the importance of Gratitude at the same time as they learn to speak.

Write below any notes or observations

INTRODUCING GRATITUDE TO CHILDREN AGED 2-5

INTRODUCTION

Gratitude for very young children is expressed as physical things they enjoy doing, people they like, particular toys or food. They will enjoy telling you about the things they like doing, or the people they like being with.

The focus on Gratitude at this age is on recognition and learning to say 'thank you'. This takes a long time to learn and involves large amounts of repetition from the adults. At this stage of development saying 'thank you' is rote, but by linking it with activities they enjoy you are training their brain.

EXPLAINING GRATITUDE TO YOUR CHILD

For young children the concept of Gratitude is hard to explain, so in practice you will find yourself talking to your child about the things they enjoy doing. Help them to know the people they love and the pets they have. Tell them as you do your Gratitude activity the reason you do this is so that they can think about all of the wonderful things they have, even when life is hard the wonderful things are still there.

Initially you will explain Gratitude in terms of being polite to people who have given you things. They will have learned the importance of reciprocity through their relationship with you as an infant and the games you played. This is the basis of the ritual of saying 'thank you' – that we received something in the first place.

The practice of Gratitude is about saying thank you for positive things in our lives. This is dependent on being able to recognise the things we like and also recognising reciprocity. These factors are the focus at this age, as they enjoy activities, or see people they like, teach your child to say 'thank you.'

ACTIVITIES TO INTRODUCE GRATITUDE

From toddlerhood upwards, encourage your child to show you things they like doing, to ask to play games they enjoy. Reply with a 'thank you' before playing them.

As they become more aware of the importance of expressing Gratitude, then encourage your child to say 'thank you' after activities they enjoy.

As your child begins to draw get them into the habit of drawing things, people or animals they like. If done frequently, daily if possible, this habit prepares them for Gratitude practices in the future.

As they grow older, form part of your family's daily routine into drawing (or writing) something they've enjoyed in the day. This works best before bed time as an opportunity to reflect on the things they've done throughout the day, so consider moving to a Gratitude Journal by the age of 4 or 5 for them to use.

One word of warning here – don't begin by asking your child what they've done in the day, this frequently results in a monosyllabic response. Instead, snuggle down with your child in bed or on the sofa. Tell them something you enjoyed about the day. Ask your child if they've had a good day. Whichever way they reply, ask them what they liked about today – this teaches their developing mind that there are always positive things, even when things overwhelm us. When they give you a response say 'thank you' and if they are old enough, get them to record it in their Gratitude Journal.

MOVING FORWARD

During this stage of a child's life it is important to build Gratitude into a ritual. A ritual is a habit that we've done so often we don't even think about it anymore.

As they become more familiar in the routine, extend their Gratitude to include more than one thing. You may choose to make it a game where you take it in turns to decide what you should draw.

Gratitude themes you may choose:
- Friends
- Animals
- Colours
- Books
- Films
- Music
- Teachers
- Places.

Apart from setting the expectation of Gratitude and thanks at this stage of a child's life you should not expect to encounter any blocks in the practice of Gratitude.

Make a note of other themes/concepts you want to try

Write below any notes or observations

INTRODUCING GRATITUDE TO CHILDREN AGED 5-7

INTRODUCTION

During this period of a child's life they use an external monologue to help them through activities. As they approach 7 or 8 this becomes internalised and eventually becomes the reflective conscious. However, at younger ages, they are likely to still require a conversation to help them reflect and identify the things they are thankful for.

At this stage of Gratitude, children can move onto Gratitude Journals regularly. Gratitude can also be separated from Special Moments of the Day, as the children learn to recognise the things they are grateful for as different from the things they enjoyed doing.

EXPLAINING GRATITUDE TO YOUR CHILD

By this age, children will have begun to have views on things that they enjoy and those that they don't. Maybe they'll get upset about social difficulties as they learn the important social etiquette rules that develop at this stage.

It's therefore helpful to introduce Gratitude as something that helps you be positive even when something has upset you. Gratitude is about remembering all the good things in our lives that we enjoy. By writing or drawing them, we are saying thank you for the positive things in our lives. That way, even when we are tired, upset or angry we can choose to remember the good things we have.

ACTIVITIES TO INTRODUCE GRATITUDE

Snuggle down with your child in bed or on the sofa, get a calm environment with minimal risk of interruption and background noise (like the television) off or down low. This calming and togetherness before beginning Gratitude is important. As they get older they'll be able to calm themselves, however at this age your physical presence as you sit and breathe deeply will help your child to do the same. Both of you close your eyes and take five deep slow breaths to relax your bodies and minds.

Tell them something you enjoyed about the day. Ask your child if they've had a good day. Whichever way they reply, ask them what they liked about today – this teaches their developing mind that there are always positive things, even when things overwhelm us. When they give you a response say 'thank you' and get them to record it as their Special Moment of the Day.

Ask them what things in their lives that they really like today. You are likely to get some varied answers from your child and if they are genuine things that they can be appreciative for having then thank your child. It is only with age that we inhibit our minds.

Now is the time to record these in the Gratitude Journal. Whether your child draws or writes is their choice, the act is of more significance. It may help them to focus to do this in silence, although initially you may find you give them encouragement to record their Gratitude and Special Moment of the Day.

Only after they have finished is it right to let them describe or discuss what they have recorded. It can be very tempting to interact with your child as they record their Gratitude, however this can influence their focus. Thank your child for what they have shared and ensure they respond with a "thank you."

MOVING FORWARD

This routine will develop over time, as your child becomes more familiar with reflecting on their day, there will be less focus on the conversation to identify what they are grateful for and more time spent on independent recording in their Gratitude Journal. This will in turn increase the number of things they are able to record in their journals each day, building to four or five by the time they are seven.

As a child approaches seven, there will also be a shift in their level of reflection. This is due to the conscious beginning to develop and so the thought process that has had to be externalised for so many years (the child's commentary) begins to internalise. For the child this means they move from needing to talk through their Gratitude, to being in a position where they will think about it and tell you the things they choose.

On different weeks you may choose to think about particular themes for Gratitude, these might include:
- Friends
- Games
- Interests
- Holidays
- Places
- Characters
- Books
- Learning.

At this stage it is important to make Gratitude a fun reflective time. If you encounter blocks or repeated focus on negative experiences, then suggest positives from the day to focus on instead.

📝 Make a note of other themes/concepts you want to try

Write below any notes or observations

INTRODUCING GRATITUDE TO CHILDREN AGED 8-12

INTRODUCTION

This stage of a child's life is an amazing period, a child learns to be an independent social being and their internal thought process gradually becomes a conscience. A child's personality takes off and their ability to give opinions (normally based on the opinions on the adults in their lives) opens up all sorts of conversations.

Gratitude during this age range will begin to move from what they think they should say, to the things they have enjoyed or are thankful for. This can be very different from Gratitude at younger ages. Gratitude Journals should begin to become personal, almost like a diary, during this age range and so it will become something that a child can choose to share with their parents, rather than the parent instigating the Gratitude.

As they approach the onset of puberty, it is important for the developing brain that your child has as many new activities or experiences as they can. This will quickly be reflected in their Gratitude and you'll see them write about some of the new things they've tried.

EXPLAINING GRATITUDE TO YOUR CHILD

During this stage of a child's life they have developed a personality and character of their own, they begin to make their mind up about friendships and choices about things they want to do in their lives, for example this is the stage where we see them say they want to be a such and such. These decisions are based on the experience and values of the adults in their lives, so it is important to introduce Gratitude well.

Start by talking about the things your child loves doing and who their friends are. Explain that Gratitude is about celebrating the wonderful things in our lives every day. By saying thank you for the things we enjoy, we are showing that we appreciate them. Many people feel more positive and happier after they've been sharing the things they feel appreciative of.

Every day we will write or draw in our special Gratitude Journals. These are books that we use to celebrate the things we like having or doing. The Gratitude Journals must be treated with respect and looked after.

Show your child Examples 1-3 at the start of the book and discuss what the children have done in theirs.

ACTIVITIES TO INTRODUCE GRATITUDE

Make daily Gratitude time a special time with your child: sit together and discuss what they will record before they write in their Gratitude Journals. Minimise disruptions, do it somewhere quiet where you can have this special time together.

Explain that in order to start Gratitude it helps to clear our minds. Ask them to close their eyes and see all of the thoughts going on in their heads. Imagine all those thoughts sitting in balloons. Now as you both take five deep slow breaths, imagine blowing out the balloons. Breathe in through your nose, pause and then breathe out through your mouth. Imagine all of those thought balloons being released as you breathe out. When they are ready they can open their eyes again.

Ask your child how they feel. Did that help them to relax?

Share with your child the things you enjoy doing and are thankful for. Ask them about the things they enjoy doing. Show them their Gratitude Journals and help them to choose their five items of Gratitude. Once they've recorded them, discuss with your child how they select a Special Moment of the Day. What activity or memory that gave them a strong emotion would they like to remember from the day? Help your child to identify and select just one to record in their Gratitude Journals.

When they finish, encourage your child to say "thank you", then sit with them with both of your eyes closed. In your heads think about the things you have just shown appreciation for, as you breathe slowly in and out as before five times. Now you can both open your eyes and end your Gratitude.

MOVING FORWARD

It is important to help your child see Gratitude as part of the daily routine. If time is short on one day, then it is better to do just one or two items of Gratitude than miss it.

At first your child will be able to record the things they enjoy doing or their family and friends in their Gratitude Journals, however, after a few days it is likely your child will struggle to generate new things to be grateful for.

At this point you may choose to adopt weekly topics to focus the Gratitude Journals into different areas, such as books or holiday activities. These could link to the seasons or you could take it in turns to draw as a family to pick the theme. Discuss Examples 4 and 5 from the start of the book, which are more concept based ways of practising Gratitude.

Themes that you may like to consider for Gratitude:
- Places
- Smells
- Emotions
- Things they can touch
- Pets
- Nature
- Sounds
- Music
- Books
- Journeys
- Things that make us laugh
- Things that make us smile
- Things we have learnt.

Some parents may encounter blocks to the Gratitude at this stage as either a child focusses on negative aspects of their life or struggles with the discipline of regular practice. For some it can help to put them in charge of the focus of Gratitude for both of you. For others it may be more about making sure Gratitude is timetabled in as part of the family routine rather than a chore. Finally, others may require an explanation of the underlying basis of Gratitude, an understanding of what they are working towards, in order to buy in to the practice.

📝 **Make a note of other themes/concepts you want to try**

Write below any notes or observations

INTRODUCING GRATITUDE TO YOUNG TEENAGERS (13-15 YEARS OLD)

INTRODUCTION

During this part of a child's life they are often going through puberty. This has a direct impact on the way they think, act and feel. Their higher function areas of the brain are reduced to occasional use and the emotional part of the brain is in charge of your child's response to many things.

This makes the practice of Gratitude very important as a coping tool for the stress and emotional roller coaster during this time. Gratitude will help ground them, reduce their stress and help them to cope with the demands of their lives. It will therefore be beneficial for them to get into the habit of doing Gratitude every day.

Due to the reduction in reflective capacity during puberty it's likely to begin with, your child will struggle with seeing the benefits of the Gratitude. This will come through persistence, you will need to encourage and support them to form the habit and as they become more used to it, expect to notice the difference and in turn help them to notice that change.

EXPLAINING GRATITUDE TO YOUR CHILD

For your child at this age, Gratitude can be a solution for something. So it is useful to suggest the practice of Gratitude as a solution to help them cope with whatever is happening in their lives. Suggest it and explain the benefits, offer to teach them how to do it and share with them what you have learned as a result of your own Gratitude journey.

or example, if your child is feeling insecure, then Gratitude will help them to feel more confident about the things they have in their lives. Likewise, if they are in a negative spiral with their friendships and finding they want to complain about their friends, then Gratitude will help them to see the positives in those relationships. If your child is feeling depressed or overwhelmed by emotion, then Gratitude will help train their brain to focus on the positives in their lives.

Show them the examples of Gratitude at the start of this book and discuss them. What was each person focusing on? How could that have helped them?

ACTIVITIES TO INTRODUCE GRATITUDE

Get your child to sit with their feet firmly on the floor. Say "in preparation for Gratitude, you need to clear your mind. Close your eyes and take a deep breath. Feel the firmness through your feet and legs, let them ground you to the floor. Now I want you to imagine you are looking at the thoughts inside your head. Imagine them as balloons." Ask them to breathe in and out slowly five times. Between each breath say "imagine letting each of the balloons go and you see your thoughts float off into the distance." Now they can open their eyes.

Ask them to think of five things that they are grateful for right now. Don't think too long about them, say the things that immediately pop into their heads. If your child can't think, then ask them about different aspects of their lives, like friends, family, school, hobbies. Ask them about a Special Moment in the last day that they would want to preserve as a lasting memory. These can all be entered into their Gratitude Journals.

In the first few Gratitude sessions it is normally easy to come up with more than five, however over time as Gratitude becomes more engrained and people try to not repeat themselves it becomes more challenging for those things to bubble to the surface. The clearing exercise at the beginning of this section will help with that.

Get your child to read their Gratitude statements, and focus on the positive feelings that accompany them. Feel that sense of satisfaction with being appreciative.

Ask them to close their eyes and hold that feeling for five slow breaths. By the fifth breath they should feel a shift in their body and possibly feel more relaxed. When they do, encourage them to think of the things they are looking forward to in the day ahead.

MOVING FORWARD

As you move forwards with your child, ensure that the Gratitude continues. If time is short on one day, then it is better for your child to do just one or two items of Gratitude than miss it. They can try the different visualisation exercises described in the chapter on Helping Someone Let Go of their Thoughts.

Explain to your child that it's only after 4-6 weeks that they'll notice the benefit and although it's hard, it is important to keep going. Share with them the chapter on Tricks the Brain Will Play on You from the beginning of the book.

As they become more familiar with the practice, they should begin to take responsibility for their own Gratitude and developing it. You should see the conversations become more reflective about the practice of Gratitude and less about what to write.

Concepts that you may like to consider for Gratitude:
- Memories
- Friendship
- Community
- Learning
- Optimism
- Curiosity
- Excitement
- Rewarding
- Entertaining
- Contentment
- Enjoying the moment.

Stress and negativity are parts of the growing teenager's brain during this stage. It is important that you remember the changes going on in the brain and help to make the formation of the habit stress free. Explain what you want to help them achieve, help them to understand what is happening in their brain and why Gratitude is important. Suggest ways of making it a hassle free part of their routine and things they could include. Respect their privacy by talking to them about how they are finding it rather than what they are writing down, if they want to share they will. Over time they will want to explore the practice of Gratitude.

Make a note of other themes/concepts you want to try

Write below any notes or observations

INTRODUCING GRATITUDE TO TEENAGERS 15 AND OLDER

INTRODUCTION

This age is a wonderful time in the development of our child. As they emerge from puberty their brains reconnect the higher function areas and they experience a learning spurt. At this time, for the first time in their lives, they develop their own value and belief systems. This is important, as up until this age they have tended to follow the values of you, their teachers or other adults in their lives, this coming of age gives them the chance to make their own minds up about what they want to choose to believe.

For your child, they will need to see the need to choose to commit to Gratitude, maybe they will need the verification of hearing your experiences; maybe they will need to see the famous people who practise Gratitude; maybe they will need to try it for three months. It may be that you choose to both keep Gratitude Journals and do it together each day or compare notes, whichever method helps your child to see the benefits and choose to make it part of their emerging young adult life.

EXPLAINING GRATITUDE TO YOUR CHILD

Many successful people have made Gratitude part of their daily lives. They see it as part of what makes them successful, they believe that by focussing on the positives in your life, you attract more positives into your life. By taking the time to express your Gratitude to other people, they are making others feel more positive.

Gratitude can often be a coping mechanism for dealing with life's stresses. When we're feeling overwhelmed or emotionally drained, it focusses our mind back on the things we have in abundance in our lives. This makes the brain feel more positive about the situation and helps you to cope with whatever is going on. The positive effects of Gratitude have even been studied by universities.

Gratitude involves spending 5-20 minutes a day reflecting on the things you are grateful for in your life and the Special Moments that you want to cherish. These are often recorded in a special journal so that at times of hardship or stress you can read them and experience the positive feelings from the Gratitude.

Show them the examples of Gratitude at the start of this book and discuss them. What was each person focussing on? How could that have helped them?

ACTIVITIES TO INTRODUCE GRATITUDE

Ask your teen to sit with their feet firmly on the floor. Say "in preparation for Gratitude, let's clear our minds. Close your eyes and feel your feet on the solid floor, now feel your legs connected to your feet and the ground. Breathe in and out as you feel your body relax. Now I want you to imagine your thoughts as balloons." Ask them to breathe in and out slowly. Between each breath say "imagine letting each of the balloons go and you see your thoughts float off into the distance. After you feel the shift in your body, take one more breath and open your eyes."

Ask them to think of five things that they want to show appreciation for. With a clear mind it helps to focus on the feeling of Gratitude and watch the things ride up in their minds, rather than try to think "what am I grateful for?" Ask them about a Special Moment in the last day that they would want to preserve as a lasting memory. These can all be entered into their Gratitude Journals.

In the first few Gratitude sessions it is normal to experience an abundance of things to be grateful for. Over time many people choose to focus on what they feel grateful for at that time, whilst others choose to focus on new things each day, taking time to not repeat themselves.

Ask them to close their eyes once more and focus on how grateful they feel about the world around them. As they breathe slowly in and out, feel the positivity soak through their bodies, preparing their bodies for the ability to cope with the success and the challenges in the day ahead. Encourage them to hold this moment until they feel a physical shift in their bodies.

Reflect on the things they have achieved and the things they will achieve in the next day. When they are facing challenge their bodies feel able to face it with Gratitude, even if it is for the learning opportunity that situation has given them. As they open their eyes leave their Gratitude with a smile as they feel the potential for another wonderful day.

MOVING FORWARD

As your child moves forward with their practice, ensure that they continue the daily Gratitude sessions. Help them to understand that even if time is short on one day, then it is better to do just one or two items of Gratitude than miss it. Focus most on the first three months of Gratitude so it becomes routine. Remember to share the suggestions from the section on Helping Someone Let Go of Their Thoughts, this will help them to find their preferred method.

As they become more familiar with the practice, they should begin to experiment with focussing on different concepts. As their Gratitude develops over the year, hold regular conversations with them about their Gratitude, allowing them to share the benefits they are finding and the impact it is having on their lives. This collaborative growth will help to ensure that Gratitude is a daily ritual that enhances their lives.

Concepts that they may like to consider for Gratitude:
- Home
- Basic needs
- Higher needs
- Optimism
- Curiosity
- Excitement
- Rewarding
- Exploration
- Contentment
- Enjoying the moment.

At this stage of your child's life, the practice of Gratitude should be about choice. To remove any blocks they may have about the practice, you may choose to share this book with them or help your child research the positive impact of Gratitude. It may be that you give them a Gratitude Journal as a gift or share yours with them. You may want to compare notes or discuss topics as you both move forward with your practice of Gratitude.

📓 **Make a note of other themes/concepts you want to try**

📝 Write below any notes or observations

THANK YOU

Finally, to end this book, I want to thank you for your commitment. Today's world is very busy and stressful and it can be hard taking time out for yourself.

Taking a few moments to be calm and relaxed throughout the day is becoming increasingly important as we are bombarded with information from the technological world around us.

By taking the time to teach these skills to your child, you are helping them to make healthy life choices in the future. They will have a reason to rest from the technology, a reason to relax and most of all a reason to be positive.

So, hard as it may be to get started, I have no doubt their future selves will be thanking you for investing in nurturing this life-changing practice.

With Gratitude,
Richard

ABOUT THE AUTHOR

Richard Daniel Curtis is an internationally renowned behaviour expert. The former teacher is known for his impact with turning around some of the most extreme behaviours and is consulted by people from around the globe. Said to have personally influenced the lives of over half a million children, Richard is passionate about helping change a generation.

He has founded The Mentoring School, a professional development training team to help people supporting children, young people, young adults, refugees, apprentices, sports coaches, business leaders and more. Richard is also the founder of multi-award winning special needs support service The Root Of It.

Author of The Curtis Scale, a tool to assess the social and emotional development of children, Richard's work has had an impact in five continents.

He has written seven books, including Gratitude in Primary Schools, Gratitude in Secondary Schools and Higher Education, Gratitude at Home, The Parent's Guide to the Modern World, 101 Tips for Parents, 101 More Tips for Parents and 101 Behaviour Tips for Parents.

Richard lives in Southampton with his girlfriend, their newborn baby boy and his pet chickens (rescued battery hens obviously).

Notes

Notes

Notes

Notes

Notes

Notes

Copyright © 2016 Richard Daniel Curtis
www.thekidcalmer.com

Printed in Great Britain
by Amazon